MW01505901

Broken Made Whole

JESUS IN IT ALL

Jill Kaczmarowski

Copyright © 2021 by Jill Kaczmarowski. All rights reserved.

The views and opinions expressed in this work are those of the author and do not necessarily reflect the views and opinions of Braughler Books LLC.

This book or any portion thereof may not be reproduced or used in any manner whatsoever without the express written permission of the publisher except for the use of brief quotations in a scholarly work or book review. For permissions or further information contact Braughler Books LLC at:

info@braughlerbooks.com

Cover photo: © Kevin Carden | Dreamstime.com

Scriptures marked AMP taken from the Holy Bible, Amplified Bible (AMP) Copyright © 2015 by The Lockman Foundation, La Habra, CA 90631. All rights reserved.

Scriptures marked NIV taken from the Holy Bible, New International Version®, NIV® Copyright ©1973, 1978, 1984, 2011 by Biblica, Inc.® Used by permission. All rights reserved worldwide.

Scriptures marked NKJV taken from the Holy Bible, New King James Version® Copyright © 1982 by Thomas Nelson. Used by permission. All rights reserved.

Scriptures marked NLV taken from the Holy Bible, New Life Version (NLV) Copyright © 1969, 2003 by Barbour Publishing, Inc.

Scriptures marked TPT taken from the Holy Bible, The Passion Translation®. Copyright © 2017, 2018, 2020 by Passion & Fire Ministries, Inc.

Printed in the United States of America
Published by Braughler Books LLC., Springboro, Ohio

First printing, 2021

ISBN: 978-1-970063-76-9

Library of Congress Control Number: 2021919107

Ordering information: Special discounts are available on quantity purchases by bookstores, corporations, associations, and others. For details, contact the publisher at:

sales@braughlerbooks.com or at 937-58-BOOKS

For questions or comments about this book, please write to:

info@braughlerbooks.com

Braughler™
Books
braughlerbooks.com

Dedication

THIS BOOK IS DEDICATED to my loving husband and best friend. HE has supported and stood by me with unconditional love through the good, the bad, and the ugly. ALSO THIS IS FOR my two sons WHO ARE God's gift and joy in my life. And to God who saved my life! Without Him I would not be here to share my testimony and love for God, Family and Life.

Acknowledgements

To my dear friends who prayed and also helped encourage me in the beginning stages of my writing as the book began to take form.

Contents

*"Like a caterpillar that turns into a beautiful butterfly,
so can you be transformed into His beautiful daughter."*

–Jill Kaczmarowski

Introduction

Growing up with shame, guilt and feeling of abandonment was all too much for me to handle as a little girl who desired to be loved, heard and protected, who desperately wanted to feel safe in her surroundings. I knew I was missing something in my spirit that longed to be filled. I found later in my journey that only God could fill that place. In the darkest moments of my addiction I was brought to my knees, where Jesus showed up rescuing me and bringing me into His perfect love. It was through the pain and brokenness of my heart that He gave me His and began to change me. We all have a story that God wants to shine thorough us so we can walk serving Him with our testimony that will help change a life. This is mine.

The Lord is close to the brokenhearted and saves those who are crushed in spirit. (Psalm 34:18 NIV)

Through my own struggles growing up in a broken home, rebellion and addiction as a teen, I have answered the call on my life dedicated to helping women and teenage girls find hope, healing and freedom only found in Christ Jesus. It is in the personal relationship I have developed with JESUS, that HIS love, grace and LIVING WORD transformed me. I believe when we truly surrender our hearts we are set FREE to walk in Love. I have such a love for God that in my story you can hear His Love for me, as He brought me out of darkness and into His glorious light. I am ever thankful for all He has done and continues to do! Truly without Him I would not be here to share my story of hope.

Today as a Christian woman, I have a deep desire and passion to help others discover their true identity and love for Christ as they find the courage to walk through the storms of life where Jesus wants to meet us. My heart and passion to share my story is in the hope that it will encourage and empower you to grow into the beautiful, strong, and confident women you were created to be.

Gods has a calling on your life and is inviting you to accept His salvation and love that He wants to pour over you.

CHAPTER 1

The Struggle

For a long time, I believed I could never live without you. I felt I would always need you in my life to take away the pain and the sorrow. I was deceived, thinking that I needed you in order to have fun. When I was with you, I felt confident, beautiful, and courageous—my low self-esteem was gone. I believed in you, trusted you, but you betrayed me. You told me you would always be there for me, and I believed you. I wanted to hear and believe your truth rather than what I needed to hear, the truth about the lies and the destructive path you were taking me down.

Most days you enticed me to play and have fun because you wanted my undivided attention, but that pulled me away from my loved ones and the things that were important to me. You made sure I felt awful the next morning, so I was unable to function and make it to work. You never wanted the best for me. You caused me to lie, steal, and hurt the people I loved.

I still stuck around thinking I was in love with you. I tried to change my number, but you always managed to find a way back. You brought nothing but misery and destruction to my life. I sold my soul and became a captive of yours; doing everything you wanted me to. You ruled over me and became my god. Because of you, I found myself on the streets using every day, finding ways to support my habit.

You caused me to be raped, beaten, and robbed. I can only hope one day you will be alone and feel the misery you brought me. You were my drug addiction, and you quickly brought me to my knees.

I wrote this letter for my graduation night after six months of treatment. It was a healing moment.

This is my story of transformation and redemption. As a little girl I was searching to find love and acceptance in the brokenness and emotional trauma caused by my parents' divorce and the struggles I had with my mom. The pain was too great to bear for an eight-year-old child. I lost my voice trying to make sense of my emotions, because I had no one and no way to express my thoughts. I was told how to feel and at times felt nothing at all.

When my dad left I felt abandoned, unloved, and unwanted. I became numb and lost seeking love in all the wrong places. The only way I knew to cope was to escape reality by pretending I was someone else. When among my friends and their families, I pretended their life was my own. I created a fantasy of belonging that was nonexistent. I began to believe the negative thoughts in my head that told me I was not good enough or worthy to be loved. I wanted to be someone else, anyone else. I turned to alcohol, drugs, and men to escape but that only fueled even more lies and negative thoughts. I was desperate to belong.

Before the divorce my home was like most homes. Dad worked hard and traveled as a Jewish comedian to the Catskill Mountains, where he was well known for his performances. Mom kept the house and took care of my older brother and me. My dad traveled so much that my parents began to grow apart. The fighting and arguing started, and before long Dad moved out.

Dad moved to New York and we stayed in Florida. The only time I got to see my dad was over the summer. I was only eight and filled with emotions I didn't understand. I had always been Daddy's little girl. Did I do something wrong? What caused mom and dad to stop loving each other and fighting for our family? I never knew the whole truth but had to accept they were not getting back together.

In spite of the heartache I knew I had to move forward. I learned to smile while, inside, I was dying. I put on a good mask and hid my tears. It was exhausting. Home was no longer a place of comfort. I wanted to be loved, protected and accepted. I wanted a family and a loving home like my friends. My home was not that place anymore. I was so young and didn't realize that other families had struggles. I thought we were the only failed family.

Many nights I cried myself to sleep because I missed my father, but most of it became a blur as I blocked out the pain. When my dad first left it was hard on my mom. She had to work long hours, had no car, and two children to take care of. The stress and the emotional pain caused her to lose hope and motivation. Some nights I could hear the cries from her room.

Over time her drinking increased. She became depressed, short-tempered, and abusive. Her pain became so unbearable that she tried to take her life. Thank God, she never succeeded. I know my mom did her best to care for my brother and me. We never went hungry and always had a roof over our heads. Some of my fondest moments as a child were the wonderful aromas when she cooked. Yet it was hard to appreciate. I had the essentials but felt emotionally disconnected from my mom. Her attempts to love me were hard to receive. I was angry with my mom, blaming her for breaking up our family. Later I learned she was not to blame. My dad had decided to leave us.

Slowly my heart began to harden. I tried to be a good girl, but felt I had to behave a certain way to get her love and approval. When seeing other families play games, go to the park, or attend their child's sporting events, it broke another piece of my heart because we were not that family. I remember a time I successfully begged to try out for the high school cheerleading team, a sport I loved. I actually made it and became the co-captain of the team, but my mom never came to any of our games or competitions. This multiplied my pain of not having the supportive family I longed for.

My mother and I began to argue all the time. After school I had to go straight home to do chores. It became more important to go the grocery store down the street than to do my homework. I resented my mom for the pressure she put on me when I was the child and she was the parent.

Then my mom did not work and spent most of her days in bed. We lived in a one-bedroom apartment. My brother and I had to share the couch bed. I always dreamed of having my own room. Anytime I was invited, I slept over at my friend's home. There was no personal space for me, and my anger and frustration grew. She became verbally abusive, and I got more rebellious. I felt like a prisoner in my home, robbed of my childhood, unable to do anything. It got to a point I couldn't handle it anymore. All I wanted was to be a child. At the age of fourteen I decided to run away, and that's when I discovered the true horrors that awaited a naïve little girl like me.

The parents of a friend knew my struggles at home and decided to let me stay with them, but that turned out to be a mess. My mom reported them to Child Care Services because I was a minor and would not come home. One day the police showed up. It was a scary day—five police officers for one little girl!

I was put in the state's custody and taken to a foster home while the allegations I made about my mom being abusive were investigated. Oh my, that was no home! We were six girls stuffed in one room, one bathroom, and a house that was never cleaned. I hated it, and again I felt something was missing. It was a confusing time for me, yet I refused to go home. That began a battle for my mom to fight to bring me home.

A few weeks later my mom was summoned to court. Facing my mom in court was hard, and today I know it broke her heart. While the courts investigated my mom and my reasons for running away, my friend's parents were able to get temporary custody of me.

I thought I was in a loving home, but again I found a false love. They took me in, showering me with material things, only for me to find out the husband had predatory ideas to assault me, and he did. Most of it was a blur. After several months the courts sent me back home to my mother's. I still did not want to go back home, but as a minor I had no choice.

I was angry at my mom for the way she treated me. The verbal abuse and sometimes physical abuse caused me to act out from a wounded heart, and once home the arguing began again. I was frustrated at the lack of a stable home environment that a child needs. In her pain she could only see how the divorce affected her and could not see how difficult it was for my brother and me. At sixteen I decided to leave home again, never to return, with the thought that I would be better on my own.

. . . .

Going Deeper—The Struggle

What part of your struggle causes you to walk with a wounded heart?

Do you feel as if your family is or has failed you? How?

Are you ready to go deeper with God and turn it over to him, allowing the healing to begin? What is one thing you can turn over today?

PRAYER

God, fill me with your love and bring healing to the broken place in my heart. I come before you asking for your help to change me from the inside out so I can become the person you created me to be. I pray that you teach me how to open my heart so that I can receive your love. I lift this prayer up to you in your mighty name, Jesus. Amen.

He heals the brokenhearted and binds up their wounds (Psalm 147:3 NKJV).

NOTES

CHAPTER 2

Broken

A boy I was dating at the time had an uncle with an apartment for rent. He let me stay in the apartment for free for the first two months. With their help, I got a job and began night classes to take my GED. I had a desire and a determination to make something of my life. I never wanted to feel lost in the pain my mom went through with her divorce. It was the first time I felt free and was able to take care of myself.

But still something was missing. It was lonely and hard at first, working and going to school. I had to grow up so fast. I longed to be in a home with a mom and dad. I missed my family. There was a force inside me that kept me strong, determined and able to face what was in front of me. The lies were louder than God at this point. Eventually my emotions and the negative thoughts in my head got the best of me. I slowly started down the wrong path, again trying to fill the missing piece. This time was different because I was on my own.

I began drinking and staying out late, not showing up for work, missing my rent payments and experimenting with strong drugs like crack cocaine. At first I thought it was fun and harmless but soon realized the destruction it could cause in my life. My mind never stopped racing, constantly tormenting me with negative thoughts about myself. I had very low self-esteem—never feeling good enough, smart enough, or pretty enough. When I was high, I could escape and fill in the missing pieces. My thoughts slowed down, and I could be someone other than myself. I felt like everything was okay; or so I thought.

Men became a weakness. I was able to manipulate and take advantage of them to get my needs met, and they in turn took advantage of me. But I did not care. I began to compromise my morals and values. I did things and acted out in ways I never could image just to keep the high alive.

When with a man I replaced the negative thoughts with a false sense of feeling smart enough, pretty enough, and worthy enough to be loved, while supporting my bad habits. For a brief time I no longer felt insecure. I felt powerful, not recognizing I was actually powerless and deceived.

I got to a point where I was losing everything including my self-respect and dignity. I wanted to run and start a new life somewhere, but you can't run and hide from yourself. I feared if I stopped running, I would have to feel all the pain! The pain of my parents' divorce and growing up in a broken home led to my addiction that covered up the pain and allowed me to live in a false reality. The pain brought me to places no respectable girl should go. The pain became so debilitating; it caused me to give up and try to take my life. The shame was unbearable. There were so many days I felt empty and alone, even when I was not alone.

I was at a point of no return and knew I had to make a change. The path I was on was leading to self-destruction and, eventually, to death. It was time to stop pretending to smile when inside I was dying; I had to put the mask down. That is how the enemy tries to steal, kill, and destroy us. It's subtle, and we don't see it coming. It became a loud, lying voice in my head. I believed the lies as if they were true. Those thoughts deceived me, and before I knew it, I was knocked down. I found myself in the pit, on the streets with no real place to call home. My life was falling apart. That's what happens when you don't have an anchor, like Jesus.

One dark day I reached a point where I did not want to go on any longer, but when I tried to end my life I felt a love deep inside my spirit. I did not know it was there, but it was stronger than the pain. It was like a flickering flame of a candle, and if blown out, I would not be here to share my story with you. Today I know that light was the love of Jesus. Someone somewhere was praying for me. I realized only God could be my Father and refuge, yet I was not ready to accept His way. I continued on my destructive path. I thought I could change on my own.

I didn't think things could get any worse, and yet they did. I jumped from hotel to hotel, dealer to dealer, staying up for days on end without eating or drinking. I didn't even recognize myself in the mirror. Who was I becoming? What was becoming of my life?

The high I chased no longer replaced the pain. Now it *was* the pain. I was carrying a ball and chain. I was a slave to my addiction. I just wanted the nightmare to end. One desperate day I cried out in a hotel by the side of a toilet, high and paranoid by the drug that had its hold on me. "Lord! If You are there, I need to know who You are. I need Your help in this moment! Please make it all stop!" I remember crawling to Him. "I can't go on like this anymore." I did not know God, but I knew of Him. I had heard people talk about the joy and peace they found in Him and how His strength brought freedom that changed their lives. I wanted that so badly! But how could He love someone like me after all that I have done? My addiction caused me to do many things I was ashamed of. God heard my cry and showed up that night.

Suddenly warmth came over me, and I felt His presence as He wrapped His loving arms around me. I heard His gentle, sweet and kind voice say, "You are not alone. I am with you. Run to me and I will give you a new life." I was desperate and wanted to change. I just didn't know how to turn from my path of destruction to a path of victory in Christ Jesus, but He did! He wanted to teach me. He wanted me to love myself as He sees and loves me no matter what my past held. Most of all He wanted to tear down the walls I had built over my heart and heal the wounds so I could receive ALL the love He had for me. He wanted to invite me on a journey with Him to a life of freedom discovering who He is and wants to be for me.

When I look back it was through the storms and heartache that I found my greatest victories, which have given me the willingness to overcome and not give up. I know how hard it can be to walk in the pain and struggles of life. In the agony of my pain and tears, the ONLY way through was with Jesus.

Some days He holds my hand and pulls me along, while on other days He holds me in His arms and tells me everything is going to be okay. That night I checked myself into treatment for the fourth time. I had tried too many times to change on my own, which never worked. My prior visits to treatment were twenty-eight days long, which didn't give me the foundation and strength to continue to stay the course.

I committed to a six-month program, knowing it was my last chance to save my life. That's when my journey with Jesus began. One night I was introduced to Jesus in one of our group therapy sessions. My eyes began to open, and I experienced the true freedom that only comes from knowing Him. I learned that surrendering is the first step to admitting that you're powerless over your addiction and that your life is unmanageable. Surrendering meant I lost the battle and was willing to give up control.

For too long I had hidden behind fear and tried to control everything in my life so I could feel safe and protected. It had become easier to live from my brokenness that kept me from seeing the truth and chaos in my life. Finding the courage to admit I was powerless and needed help was scary. I was exhausted, worn out, and beaten down. I was desperate and ready to change. It took some time for me to surrender my heart, but my mind was willing. I had to believe God was with me every step of the way, even in my addiction.

God is with us in our struggles and our heartaches. When we begin to grow weary in the battle, He knows our pain, fear, and loneliness. When we meet God in the storm, He is faithful to see us through and guide our every step. When we invite God into that place of fear and the unknown, we are never alone. ***Know that His word tells us when we are weak He wants to be strong for us*** (2 Corinthians 12:10 NKJV).

The enemy would love to keep us distracted by encouraging us to keep running and cover our hurts with worldly and fleshly desires. Instead, I chose to go through the storm into the arms of Jesus. It was in the storm where Jesus met me. I realized He did not need anything from me. He is all-sufficient.

What He wants and longs for is our love and affection. He desires a personal relationship with us. There is no cost to be with Jesus. I began to discover who God says I am. I was not who the drugs caused me to become. I was worth something and started to see glimpses of the sweet little girl God created me to be. He began to wrap me in His gentle, kind, and compassionate heart in order to convict me and not condemn me. His love wanted to set me free.

The shame, guilt, and condemnation He revealed are not the works of the cross. They are the works of the enemy, who only wants to cause me to live with unbelief and torment, producing an attitude of mistake and failure over my thoughts and inner self.

Before leaving treatment, I made a decision to surrender my life to Him. I responded to His invitation, accepting Him as my Lord and Savior. It was confusing at first, but I knew in my spirit I was going to be okay. From that day on I have not stopped running into His loving arms, seeking to know more of Him and His word which has transformed me from the inside out.

Jesus began to heal me with His love and His word. I realized I did not have to hide from Him any longer. He wanted me to come as I was—broken—so He could make me whole and give me a life worth living. *I came that you might have life, and have it in abundance to the full, till it overflows* (John 10:10 AMP).

If you are reading this from a broken place and want to change, recommit, or go higher with the Lord in your maturity, take that step and fight back. Repent! Get ready to get in the ring and battle for your life. You are worth it. God wants to heal every part of our hearts, taking the pain we have endured and replacing it with His joy and strength. *The joy of the Lord is your strength* (Nehemiah 8:10 NKJV). When we can be honest with ourselves and accept the brokenness in us we can find the hope of Jesus who restores our life, transforms our mind and renews our wounded hearts.

After treatment I started to attend Narcotics Anonymous meetings. My boyfriend, who later became my husband, was very supportive of my healing and my continued treatment. He stood by my side through it all. There was much healing in our relationship, too. He was patient and nurturing through my recovery process, showing me unconditional love like no one else ever had.

There were moments in our relationship that he witnessed my destructive behavior caused by my addiction. When his heart was breaking, he gave me an ultimatum: treatment or our relationship was over. He could not watch me kill myself, and I couldn't bear to lose the man I loved.

It was that love he showed me that saved my life. He believed in me when I couldn't believe in myself. He saw the wonderful women I could become. It was through my darling husband's loving confidence and God's offer of rescue that I found my way back.

I started discovering more of who I am with the help of God, my husband, and the Twelve-Step program. After two years, we were engaged and got married. Our wedding day was one of the happiest days of my life. I felt like a princess, so loved and desired—not for what I could offer, but for who I was. My whole life I had dreamed of having a family of my own, being a wife and a mom—that dream was coming true. Someone like me found love!

When I first met my husband at work, I was immediately drawn to him. He is handsome, kind, gentle, and the most considerate person I have ever met. He has a wonderful smile and a big heart. He always brings laughter into my life. It was all so surreal at first for me. I still had lies in my head that I was to silence. But I knew with hard work, dedication, and the hope of God, all things are possible with Him. ***What seems impossible to you is never impossible to God*** (Matthew 19:26 TPT).

Life has not been perfect, and we've had our ups and downs, but through it all Love Conquered! God continues to teach me how to love others without expectations, accepting that no one owes me anything. Selfless love gives us the freedom to truly put others first, becoming devoted to one another in love. ***Be devoted to one another in love. Honor one another above yourselves*** (Romans 12:10 NIV).

. . . .

Going Deeper—Broken

When you hear the word broken what resonates with you?

What mask if any are you hiding behind to hide your brokenness?

Are you worn out trying to be something that you're not? Write out your why?

What is one step you can take today to lower or remove your mask and allow God to fill that place?

Pain can cause us to give up, or it can motivate us to walk through and persevere to the other side where healing and breakthrough come. We all have a bottom that causes us to be desperate and want to change. I hit rock bottom, and the only way out was to look up and find Jesus. Jesus showed up and poured His love into my heart and began to change me. He wanted to bring joy to my life when the pain and sadness was too much to bear. He wanted to be my strength, when I wanted to give up and end my life. It's in the storms where we learn to lean on Him as we grow. They are teachable moments if we can open our hearts and remain teachable. What part of your pain has or will motivate you to persevere through the storm so you can find the healing that awaits you in Jesus Christ?

PRAYER

God, guide me to know that you are the missing piece that can restore my pain. Help me to walk in your strength so I can be FREE, no longer held captive in the storm of my brokenness. Bring me back to your purpose and the plans you have always had for me. In your precious name, I thank you, Jesus. Amen.

For I know the plans I have for you, declares the Lord, plans to prosper you and not to harm you, plans to give you hope and a future (Jeremiah 29:11 NIV).

NOTES

NOTES

CHAPTER 3

Mending

My whole life I dreamed of being a mom. Now that I was, I had so many doubts. I was so full of God; love of my husband. I grew healthy in my recovery. Yet it all seemed to dissolve. Motherhood brought love and joy into my heart that words could not express, yet I still felt empty inside. The fears and lies returned, and I doubted my ability to love and care for a child. Will I know how? Will I know what to do? Can I love this child when I'm not sure I love myself?

Before we can love ourselves and others, we need to know what love is or even what it looks like. Growing up I rarely saw the side of love that was nurturing, unconditional, forgiving, and protective. Jesus showed what His love was and taught me how to love from a place that was not full of judgment and criticism. He began to teach me first how to love myself and change the negative thoughts so that I would stop being critical of myself. He had said to me at one time, "Every time I criticize myself, I criticize Him for I am created in His image." Yikes.

Faced with a baby two years later, a second child, I leaned on our greatest teacher—Jesus. How did I learn to walk in love for myself? First it was a decision to want to change and then to seek Jesus to help me in that change. I was desperate and no longer wanted to spend nights crying, days filled with depression, and moments of anger or fear that would come over me.

Healing takes vulnerability, honesty, and a teachable heart. Finding a safe place and someone you can trust to share your pain and confess your secret fears is important in the healing process. God's word, the Bible, tells us to **confess our sins one to another and pray for one another that you may be healed** (James 5:16 NKJV). I found that place at first to be the Twelve Step program of Narcotics Anonymous. It provided me with the tools to help me in the process of healing my wounded heart, helping me to change. God, the Bible, and Narcotics Anonymous taught me to grow in ways I never imagined I could. I started to discover who I really was and wanted to become. I no longer wanted to hide from my inner self.

The more time I spent with God in His word, the more I began to develop and grow in a close relationship with Him. But as a working mom running a household that was becoming a challenge. I was tired, irritable, and worn out. I knew I needed to find some quiet time, some me time, some God time. I needed to be recharged and refreshed, which would only come from being with God and in His word.

How was I going to find precious quiet time for God and me? I already could not handle doing everything. It took baby steps. It took practice. It took being intentional and asking my husband or a friend for help. I had to give myself permission to rest, to not always feel the pressure of having to do a task. It took asking God to orchestrate my time so I could find His balance in it all. When left up to me, it was not working. I began to lift up my calendar daily to the Lord. We came up with a game plan to mark out precious time together, work, and family.

I began to practice this daily, being intentional to make it happen. I still to this day practice this, allowing God to be in control. This has taught me to slow down, be still, breathe, and go with the flow when things don't go according to my plan. It is in the precious time I have with God where I find His peace, joy, hope, and strength that fills me up to do this thing called life. That allows me to enter His rest no matter where or what I am going through.

Some days I struggle to sit still as I am distracted by the noise of the world and the many responsibilities we have with work, family and home. Some days I find myself running into the Father's arms where He embraces me so I can climb on His lap and snuggle under His wing. There I can take a deep breath and know I'm going to be okay. It has taken time for me to learn to live from a place of peace, resting in Him, connecting spirit to spirit. This has been a journey to walk alongside Him daily as we talk, sing, and laugh. I am determined to live my best life which was when I found Jesus.

Walking alongside Jesus I started to look at the possibility of things to come rather than the things that were. *I stopped crying out Why is this happening?* I started asking *What am I to learn from you, God? What are you teaching me?* In the trial I face. At times that was difficult, but I knew if just kept my eyes on Jesus, I would make it. And I do! Some days are better than others, but with His help and strength, I do get through.

Some days my prayers are just uttering the name Jesus over and over. There is power in His name, and when I would call out *Jesus* it would fill me with His Peace. Later I learned He is the Prince of Peace. **He will keep you in perfect peace if your mind is stayed on Him** (Isaiah 26:3). Who doesn't want more peace in their life, especially during times of turbulence when the storms come? I know I do! In fact, today I want to remain in His rest and not allow the circumstances of my life to dictate how I feel. As I continued to walk out my journey to freedom with God, I began to see the transformation taking place in me, especially in my mind. Romans 12:2 became a life changing scripture for me.

"Do not conform to the patterns of this world but be transformed by the renewing of your mind. Then you will be able to test and approve what Gods will is—His good pleasing and perfect will." (Romans 12:2. NKJ)

I would pray: Dear God, I love to be in your presence where I feel safe, secure and loved. Guide me on the days when I am feeling overwhelmed and out of sorts, beating myself up about what I should or should not do for the day. Should I have woken up earlier? Should I go work out? Should I clean the house? Should I take the kids out? Should I, should I, should I? **Oh, help me to just BREATHE and take one step at a time!** I thank you, Lord, that that you are teaching me to let go of the judgment over myself. Teach me, Lord, to love and accept myself as You do.

From God: At that moment the Lord shared with me there are no *should have, would have,* or *could have* in the Kingdom. There are only opportunities to step into obedience and allow Him to direct your path. He then proceeded to tell me to love and accept myself as He sees me; a child of GOD who is fearfully and wonderfully made Palm 139:14 created in His image. Jill you are beautiful, loving, kind, giving and compassionate.

I will teach you my ways - continue to lean on me every day as you seek Me and my Word. That is when He began to share and teach me how to walk in His ways and mend my heart with His love.

. . . .

Going Deeper—Mending

What are some ways God mended your heart? Take a moment to give Him thanks.

Are you able to walk in love for yourself? If not, what is preventing you from walking in self-love? Is it shame, guilt, hatred, critical thoughts, low self-esteem, or struggling to find forgiveness?

Allow God's love to change your perspective. Fill in the blank

I no longer walk in _____ today I choose to walk in and with God's love.

No judgment. . . . Only Love!

No guilt. . . . . Only Love!

No hatred . . . . . . Only Love!

No shame . . . . . . Only Love!

Let go of all your shame and guilt. Let Him carry your burdens and replace it with His love for you. He calls us to be a light to the world and He wants to shine bright in you for all to see His glory that transformed you. When we begin to walk in love for ourselves, we can begin to walk in love for others. Love bears all things, believes all things, hopes all things, and endures all things. Love never fails. *Three remain: faith, hope and love. But the greatest of these is love* (1 Corinthians 13:7-13 NKJ).

NOTES

CHAPTER 4

Sitting Up

When I realized I did not have to try to fit in, or to compare myself to others, I found the freedom to become who God created ME to be. WOW! When I thought there was no hope, this scripture gave me the hope that I could change my thoughts. I realized I was not crazy, and that was freeing. I learned that others struggle too. I began to change the lies and negative thoughts of who I thought I was to who God said I am. I knew I had to take it slow. Take it one day at a time. Sometimes it was hour by hour and minute by minute. Some days I had to fight off several hundred negative thoughts, and that was exhausting!

God's Word tells us to take every thought captive and make it obedient to Christ (2 Corinthians 10:5 NKJV). Simply put, change that thought. I think of it like a computer that has a virus—it needs to be reprogrammed. God knew mine needed an overhaul. My journey to freedom came in waves. Sometimes I was instantly released from something; other times the process took more time, lessons, and willingness to trust the change.

One valuable lesson learned was when I lost a job that meant everything to me. It gave my life purpose so I thought. The job was me and I was the job. I became the title of who I was and not the person who I was created to be. I fell into a depression. I was so distraught from the embarrassment of what I had done to cause me to lose my job.

I wanted to replace a lost sweater that I loved. Since I was in a managerial position in retail, I knew how to manipulate the system so I could process a return, allowing me to purchase a new one at no expense to me. We were struggling financially at the time, and I embraced a lie that the rules did not apply to me. I made my own truth. I was convinced it was harmless, and I was not stealing. Truth is always revealed.

Today I thank God He allowed truth to be known; otherwise, one lie could have led back to a path of destruction. We have to be careful we are not led astray by the little lies that can accumulate and cause us to start compromising truth. That day on my way home after getting fired, I got a ticket. That was my breaking point. That crushed me. I did not want to go on at that point.

I called my husband from my car in the garage and asked if I sit here long enough with the car on, will I just go to sleep? I did not truly want to end my life, but I was so tired and broken. I wanted to go to sleep, never wake up, and hope to end up in the arms of the Father. I ended up making an appointment for my therapist, who, after hearing the story, admitted me to the hospital.

That day I was not allowed to leave her office. My husband was told to pack a bag and come pick me up. He took me straight to the hospital. I cried the whole way there. I couldn't believe I was back at this place. My husband was so compassionate and loving. He encouraged me the whole way there, assuring me everything was going to be okay. It meant the world to me that he was by my side. He has always been my strength.

I felt like I was off to treatment again. I humbly admitted myself. I knew I needed help to find my way back. When in the hospital, I started to journal to God and cry out for His help. When the nurse first came in, she asked me to take all my clothes off and gave me a gown and a big pair of panties to put on. I chuckled and asked why. She said others have tried to strangle themselves using clothing. She also proceeded to take the phone wires off the wall and removed all other wires that were accessible.

At this time the peace of the Lord was coming over me, and I knew He was there with me. When the doctor came in, I told her I did not want to kill myself. I just wanted a place to rest and turn my mind off from all the chaos and negative thoughts that were defeating me. I explained that I knew about the psychiatric wards from visiting my brother who suffered with schizophrenia. They are not a place anyone wants to visit. The patients are usually on a sedative to keep them docile so they can cope and be maintained. It is a hard battle when you suffer with mental illness. After the doctor's assessment, she knew I was not a threat to myself and sent me home.

I fell into a depression, allowing shame and guilt to come over me. I did not leave my home for six months. Some days I barely got out of my pajamas. I felt so ashamed and condemned. The lies began to get louder in my head, telling me I was not worthy of anything. I was a failure and would never amount to anything. I knew that was not from God but from the enemy who wanted to see me end my life.

God calls us to a life full of joy, peace, strength and self control. The enemy condemns us with shame and guilt. One day after I began to cry out to the Lord, I decided the pity party was over. I no longer was going to partner with the negativity and lies that wanted to keep me in bondage. I got back into His word, started journaling again, and opened up to His love and strength to nurture me back to health.

When I look back, this crisis was the best thing ever. It caused me to look deep inside to see the woman God created me to be. It gave me the opportunity to spend time with Him and learn that my identity lies only within Him, not in a job or in my circumstances. I was able to connect with the little girl inside and see who she really was—sweet, kind, loving, strong, joyful, and full of life. I just had to start believing in who God called me to be. After being knocked down many times, I was sitting up and taking notice of all God has provided and done for me.

God is a God of progress and will gently teach us if we let Him. He wants to be part of our impossible situations and give us the ability to overcome. When we fall down, it's not considered a failure in God's eyes, but a lesson that the Lord is using to build our faith and mature our walk with Him. It's not an overnight teaching, but a daily journey.

When I intentionally walk with God, it increases my faith. With Him by my side I can do all things. I found a purpose to live. He started to open the eyes of my heart and heal the wounds. He began to share scriptures that leapt off the page and into my heart.

I realized He was not looking for me to be perfect; I was putting that pressure on myself. He was calling me to walk with Him in obedience, not perfection. ***His word tells us it's better to obey then to sacrifice***

(1 Samuel 15:22 NKJV). At first, I had no idea what that meant. I then learned my obedience to God demonstrated my love for him. I realized I had to stop the negative behavior and change my stinking thinking by not allowing my emotions, reactions, anger, and self-righteousness to rule my life anymore. Do we fall short? Absolutely, but thank God, His Word tells us every day is new.

Every day I have the opportunity to learn and change my ways. It is in the slow learning that we embrace the process to walk out and learn what we need to change about our inner self. In this fashion, we can become more like Christ, one day at a time. When I think of being more like Christ, I think of His character traits, which are listed in *Galatians 5:22-23*. They are called the Fruit of the Spirit. He is loving, full of joy and peace. He is kind and gentle, faithful, full of strength that brings self-control and patience to endure all things. It took willingness and hard work to get to where I now am in my journey. The road has been hard and bumpy but also SO rewarding. I no longer want to live with anger, resentment, and bitterness. I want to experience the joy and peace of Jesus I have seen in so many others.

I remember getting glimpses of it and telling a friend *this is boring*! She said *no*! That is what His peace feels like. I was used to living in anticipation of a crisis. I had not known, nor had I experienced, peace, contentment, or true joy. These were new emotions, and I was learning to walk in this newness of life God's way.

When we grow up a certain way, we don't know any other way. With God, we can learn His way. The more I remained thankful, the more I was able to walk in the joy of who I am, a beloved Daughter of the Most High God. When I stopped dwelling on the negative thoughts and kept my eyes on Jesus, I could let go of all fear and anxiety letting His perfect love cast out all fear (1 John 4:18). As my heart grew for Him so did my desire to be in His presence. That is now my favorite place! I love to sit at God's banquet table exchanging ideas, gaining His direction in my life.

Sit at His banquet table and pause for a minute, take a deep breath, let His presence come upon you. Feel His loving arms surround you with His peace and love. Allow His love to fill your heart and listen for His still small voice.

. . . .

Going Deeper—Sitting Up

What negative thought below has become a lie that you identify?

I am ugly	I am insecure
I am fearful	I am stupid
I am weak	I am a failure
I am unloved	I am unwanted

Look at the list of truths from God's word. Start out by choosing one at a time and replace the negative thought with who God says you are. Then write the scripture and the truth on a note card and memorize it. Let it penetrate deep in your heart and mind, allowing it to wash over you, so you no longer believe and live with the lies.

I am a child of God (**1 John 3:1**)
I am confident (**Philippians 1:6**)
I am beautiful (**Song of Songs 4:7**)
I am loved (**Romans 5:8**)
I am strong (**Deuteronomy 31:6**)
I am smart (**1 Corinthians 2:16**)
I am worthy (**Psalms 139 13-14**)
I am protected (**Psalms 91:4**)
I am not afraid (**1 John 4:18**)

PRAYER

Thank you, Lord, as I come before you with an open heart so you can teach me to replace the lies. I believe your truth of who YOU say I am. Let your truth penetrate deep into my spirit so I can walk knowing my identity lies in YOU and what your word says.

. . . .

Going Deeper—Sitting up
DECLARE WHO YOU ARE IN CHRIST

1 John 3:1 (NKJV)
Behold what manner of love the Father has bestowed on us, that we should be called children of God! Therefore the world does not know us, because it did not know Him.

Philippians 1:6 (NKJV)
Being confident of this very thing that He who has begun a good work in you will complete *it* until the day of Jesus Chris.

Song of Solomon 4:7 (NIV)
You are altogether beautiful, my love; there is no flaw in you.

Romans 5:8 (NLV)
God shows his love for us in that while we were still sinners, Christ died for us.

Deuteronomy 31:6 (NKJV)
Be strong and courageous. Do not fear or be in dread of them, for it is the Lord your God who goes with you. He will not leave you or forsake you.

1 Corinthians 2:16 (NKJV)
For "who has known the mind of the Lord that he may instruct Him?" But we have the mind of Christ.

Psalm 139:13-14 (NKJV)
For You formed my inward parts; You covered me in my mother's womb. I will praise you, for I am fearfully *and* wonderfully made; Marvelous are your works, and *that* my soul knows very well.

Psalm 91:4 (NKJV)
He shall cover you with His feathers, and under His wings you shall take refuge; His truth *shall be your* shield and buckler.

1 John 4:18 (NKJV)
There is no fear in love; but perfect love casts out fear, because fear involves torment. But he who fears has not been made perfect in love.

NOTES

CHAPTER 5

Stand Up

Prayer is an open line of communication that connects our hearts and minds with God. Simply put it is a conversation. It's a way to walk supernaturally filled up with His presence, peace, joy, and strength. Prayer has fueled my life in a way that has formed a deeper friendship with The Father God, Son Jesus, and the Holy Spirit. In my prayer time I seek to know them more. I desire to encounter their presence. I ask questions as they guide, counsel and direct my steps. I seek advice, comfort, and help in times of trouble. I let the living word of God wash over me as it transforms me daily. I also praise Him with gratitude and thanksgiving. Sometimes I sing with joy as my heart joins with His. I can stand in His presence.

At first prayer was uncomfortable and foreign. I did not know how to pray or even what to say, let alone how to hear from God. I longed to connect with my Heavenly Father but didn't know how. I would sit still some days expecting something. I would try to get on my knees and pray. I would try to pray and talk with God, but my thoughts would get scattered. I had heard from another Christian it wasn't about getting on my knees or striving to hear Him, it was sharing my heart and connecting with Him. She shared that she had a prayer chair, and every day she communed there with God. It's the same as meeting a friend for coffee or having dinner at someone's house. It's a special time to commune.

She also shared that she journaled. I asked what that was. She explained it was a way to write my thoughts out, helping my mind to slow down, so I could share and hear from God. I always hated writing in school, but I was open to anything. I wanted to know Him more! I wanted to hear His thoughts and know His heart, too. I wanted to have that intimate relationship that others talked about. I realized writing to Him was a form of prayer. I got a journal and began pouring out my heart and thoughts to Him.

That night it all changed. As I wrote and prayed to seek Him I began to see a change in me. Seeking to understand His word more gave me a sense of who He wanted to be for me. He wanted to be everything for me! Journaling became a treasured time with the Lord. He taught me to start each entry with *Dear God* as if I was writing to a friend. I was. He became my best friend and a Father who nurtured the little girl in me.

I no longer call you a servant, because a servant does not know his masters business. Instead, I have called you friends, for everything I have learned I have made know to you (John 15:15 NIV).

"I will be a Father to you, and you shall be my daughters, says the Lord almighty" (2 Corinthians 6:18 NIV).

It all began to flow so easily. In writing, I was able to share my thoughts, my day, my struggles, disappointments, as well as my accomplishments, and the joy that it was beginning to bring. I loved how I was able to share with Him as though He were sitting right next to me. It became a lifeline for me to express my emotions and allow me to process what was going on in my head and heart. It helped me to dump my negative thoughts and clear my mind, letting Jesus carry my burdens. I was able to connect with Him, Spirit to spirit.

The more I journaled, the more I sought Him and knew of His love for me, but I still could not hear from Him. I knew others who said they could hear His still small voice. I too desired that. One night I sat on my bed and started again with *Dear God*, but this time when I finished sharing, I sensed God wanted to share with me. I heard Him say *write from God*. As I paused, in my own voice, I started to hear Him speak to my heart. Oh my, the joy in the many conversations we have had and still do. This is not something that is special just for me. God wants to share with you too. It has become a practice to be in His presence and seek Him so that I can know Him more. *You will seek me and find me when you seek me with all your heart* (Jeremiah 29:13 NIV).

Learning how to be still and to quiet my mind was vital in order for me to hear from Him. I had to choose to listen, discern, and then follow His direction. One time He said to me, *In Order to Be in Action, You Must Take Action.* There were times I thought I was waiting on Him, so I thought. He was actually waiting for me to stand up, step out in faith, and trust Him. He speaks to all of us in different ways. It can be a word from someone, a Scripture, a dream, or just knowing deep in our inner spirit.

God does not waste a thing. Resting in Him is a gift. When we learn to stand in His rest, we will find His perfect peace. Learning to walk in that peace can bring us from darkness to light, from pain to glory, from despair to hope, from depression to joy. As we become willing to trust the process, He begins to transform us, peeling back the inner layers that bring healing to our brokenness. Each layer brings more healing, more faith, more hope, more trust, more forgiveness, and more LOVE! I have gained more strength to stand.

As we seek to hear His voice it is important to pray and ask for His guidance and knowledge, so that we hear from God. Wise Christian counsels is good, but always go over with God what you are considering. Other meditation styles tell you to empty your mind as you sit still. This leaves an empty space, and things not of God may sneak in, which can connect you to the enemy. Focus on God to quiet your mind. Habakkuk 2:1-3 describes the process of sitting still—using our imagination, listening to the voice from our inner spirit, and then writing what God is sharing.

As I continued to seek Him and journal my thoughts and prayers He shared so many things through the Holy Spirit to me. I learned about His loving kindness and character that shaped me into His image. He would encourage me, motivate me, guide me, and even correct me. He would listen to me as I would journal my heart's desires and prayers. Then I listened, as He shared His heart with mine. He led me to scriptures that have transformed my life. We would dance, cry, laugh, and worship during my journaling time. Sometimes I would sit in His lap and cry, letting His love nurture me. It was truly healing me from the inside out, restoring my heart to its original pureness. My favorite part of journaling is the intimate time I spend with Him listening to His guidance, so I can follow His every lead. *In all your ways acknowledge Him, and He shall direct your paths* (Proverbs 3:6 NKJV).

Jesus has taught me over the years not to overdo things. I tend to over commit. I have learned to know my limits. That way, I can stop and enjoy the precious moments in front of me as I stay in the lane He has for me. How hard that was at first! I struggled when I would think I had to be in everyone else's lane to please them. I found out others' lanes broke my peace and took me out of my true purpose. I realized that when I learned to walk in peace I would always face the same situations so I could learn what peace looked like. God teaches us slowly so we can retain it, not only in our mind but in our inner man, our heart, where we learn how to walk it out. That is how I learned to stay in my lane.

I had a dear friend who loved when I would encourage her through my writing. I had no idea how it touched her. I just wrote from my heart and shared His. She saw something more. She created a blog for me, and we named it *Butterfly Letters*. It became an outlet to write, send prayers and share the hope and love of God.

I am so grateful to her because it truly was a journey of healing and brought me closer to the Lord. Today I look back and see the path the Lord laid out, using the blog as a step toward my purpose and destiny. It opened up my heart to share His, through my testimony. I love to look back through my journals and the many conversations with the Lord, seeing the growth and maturity that He has grown me. In looking back, I saw a wonderful reminder the Lord shared with me. I would like to share a few of my blog and journal entries that were special times of prayer and intimacy between me and God. I pray it blesses you to seek and hear what He is saying to you as you embark on your journey of prayer and journaling.

. . . .

JOURNAL ENTRY
You Captivate Me—2007

Jill, My child, you are captivating. See the little girl inside spinning, twirling, and dancing with Me? Jill, you captivate me every day. Jill, you are so loved and embraced not only by Me but by many. See through My eyes the beauty and love that surrounds you. Jill, embrace all the beauty that lies in you. Jill, you are beautiful and worthy to be loved. I love you, Your Heavenly Father.

Now fill in your name and reread it.

_____, My child, you captivate me. See the little girl inside spinning, twirling and dancing with Me? _____, you captivate me every day. _____, you are so loved and embraced not only by Me but by many. See through My eyes the beauty and love that surrounds you. _____, embrace all the beauty that lies in you. _____, you are beautiful and worthy to be loved. I love you, Your Heavenly Father.

. . . .

JOURNAL ENTRY
His Love—2010

From God:

Be strong and courageous. Do not be afraid. I will be with you wherever you go (Joshua 1:9 NKJV).

Walk in the confidence knowing who you are in Me. (Jesus) Love Yourself as I love you. You are a true miracle. Don't be Ashamed of your past. You are not that person anymore and never will be. Know there is power in your story; it is your testimony of which I am for you and how you came to know Me, Jesus. It is how you gained your salvation and how you came to love me and allow me to love you. You have overcome so much with Me. Walk with me as you glorify me. *Since you were precious in My sight, you have been honored and I love you* (Isaiah 43:4).

· ·

BLOG ENTRY
Open Your Heart—2014

Dear Lord, I Thank Lord that you have guided me through the pain and heartache from the bad choices I have made. I thank you that through it all I have found a deeper relationship with you. Bring me closer, Lord! Restore my heart! Teach me your ways and help me to love you with all my heart, soul, and mind. I am learning, Lord, that my peace, joy, and contentment are not found in this world, my husband, my kids, my job, and my friends. They are only found in you! Today I open and Surrender all of my heart to You, Oh Lord, to start receiving Your Love.

Life Is Not the Absence of Pain and Suffering. It's The Presence of God's Glory.

"You shall love the Lord with all your heart, and with all your soul, and with all your mind" (Matthew 22:37 NIV).

· ·

JOURNAL ENTRY
Servants Log—11/2014

How content are you with your circumstances, with your life? With whom you have become? We can only be content and at peace when we truly surrender it all to God. We can no longer be in control. But you ask how can I do that?

We must walk in faith; follow Him and the Holy Spirit. Listen for His still small voice and walk in trust, even when we can't see it. No matter what, when we trust and turn it over to God, only He can give us perfect peace and contentment in all things. He is our prince of peace. Even in the storms of life we will walk in His perfect peace. With that comes freedom and joy to be who He created us to be, walking in our true purpose, destiny, and His perfect will for our lives.

· ·

BLOG ENTRY

Learn to Be Still—2015

When was the last time you just enjoyed the moment? A sunrise, a sunset, looking up to the sky and taking in the beauty of the clouds? Sitting quietly and listening to the birds in your back yard? Watching the rain fall from your window? Slowing down long enough to read a good book or playing, really playing and interacting with your kids? What about interacting with each other?

Some have mastered all of these, and I envy them. I am still learning every day how to be still and quiet my mind giving myself permission to enjoy and relax. I don't always have to be *on*. I'm learning to just BE and not always having to do so I can BE still in God's presence. So I can BE still in the moments where joy finds peace. So I can BE still long enough to be content. So I can BE still in the spirit and put off the desires of my flesh.

One of my favorite scriptures, I look at daily on my windowsill, reminds me to be still. ***Be Still and Know That I am God.*** In the stillness of all things, we find God. Let's practice being still and living in the moment with GOD! ***Surrender your anxiety. BE still, and know that I am God I am God above all the nations, and I am exalted throughout the whole earth*** (Psalm 46:10 TPT).

Oh, my goodness, I have to share this. God amazes me every day. He is always showing me that He is there and has my back. In fact, today has been a frustrating and trying day. When I write in my blog it brings me closer to God, and I find peace. God knew I needed to be reminded of his love. I wasn't sure where the scripture was. I grabbed my phone and went to the Bible app on my phone, and what do you know, it was the verse of the day! Thank you, Father for showing up today and every day for my life is nothing without you.

. . . .

BLOG ENTRY
Find Strength in Jesus—2015

Have you ever felt overwhelmed by so much coming at you that you weren't sure how to handle it? Questioning if you have the strength it will take to overcome? Do you sometimes feel you don't fit it?

God said this to me as I was feeling those feelings and writing to him one night in prayer. He wants us to lean on Him in all things and find strength in Him.

From God: My child, stay strong! It is my strength that lives in you. Reach for it; in it you will have the power to overcome. *Yet in all these things we are more than conquers through Him who loved us* (Romans 8:37 NKJV). The world does not understand those who are in my spirit for they live in the flesh. Do not conform to the world trying to fit in and do the things that are not walking in righteousness. Be the confident, beautiful soul that you are. Don't let others tear you down or lead you astray. Stay Strong! You are strong. You walk with my authority and can do all things in my name. When you are weak call on me, for I will be your strength. *I can do all things through Christ who strengthens me* (Philippians 4:13 NKJV)!

. . . .

BLOG ENTRY
Overcoming the Storms—2016

Storms can be a cleansing time; it's just a matter of finding the strength to walk through!

Sometimes we're excited. Sometimes we're overwhelmed. Sometimes we're at our bottom, and sometimes we're in shock of what just happened as our lives are turned upside down and we lose control. I have been in that season, where the storm has brought me to my knees and I've cried out, *Lord, help me. What am I to do? Which path am I to take? What am I to learn?* Only to hear the small quiet voice of God say, *I'm here. You are not alone. Lean on me.*

It can be confusing, and at times we question God and His will. The enemy always wants to fill us with doubt and confusion, but know that it is not of God! Truly, 2015 has been a year of heartache and loss, but I know that God is in control, and through the storm I can overcome and find peace.

What storm are you facing?

Sometimes the storms can pull you under—I have experienced that in my own life. But when I surrender and call on the name of Jesus, He is there to bring me to shore. I know how hard it can be, but as I go through the storms, they are where Jesus meets me to prepare me, train me, and allow me to grow. I have grown more and more in every storm, learning more about who I am. My faith has deepened, and I have learned to trust in the process. Sometimes we need to just sit in the storm and Be Still while we wait on God. With every storm, I have become more of who God created me to be. My light shines brighter for the world to see, and God shines brighter in me.

When you pass through the waters, I will be with you; and through the rivers, they shall not overflow you. When you walk through the fire, you shall not be burned, nor shall the flame scorch you (Isaiah 43:2 NKJV). *My child, did you think I would let you down?*

We do not always get to choose our new beginnings! We must have faith and trust that God is opening new doors which we would have never walked through had a situation not forced us. I know that at the end of every storm, my life turned out better than I could have imagined, and I got closer to my purpose. Know that it can take time, maybe years, but God has a plan, and it's always so much greater than ours. *For I know the plans I have for you...plans to prosper you and give your hope* (Jeremiah 29:11 NKJV)*!*

Don't Give Up! When you think you can't hold on, the storm will pass, and the Son (Jesus) will shine.

If you're in a season of Joy, embrace it, enjoy it, and thank God for it. If you're in the storm, know they come and go, but it is in the storm that

Jesus wants to meet you first! Today I thank God for the storms I have overcome with His great Love!

Have you ever noticed that it's through our pain and struggles that we come to know and love the hope in Christ Jesus? Are you meeting Jesus in your storm? Know that He is in the storm, waiting for you to reach out so He can bring you to shore!

God is our refuge and strength, an ever-present help in our time of need. Therefore we will not fear, though the earth gives way and the mountains fall into the heart of the sea (Psalm 46 1-2 NIV).

PRAYER

Heavenly Father, I don't have the answers for why this is happening, but I know you are there. I am ready to be brought safely to shore. I know that this is a season in my life, and with you, I can overcome. Help me to meet you in the storm and show me what I am to learn and how I need to change. Comfort me and bring peace in my life as I walk through the storm, knowing you are bringing me into your perfect will for my life.

. . . .

JOURNAL PRAYER
He Is my Everything Entry—2017

Lord, I thank you for being my refuge in time of trouble. I thank you that you have rescued me from the destruction and darkness and brought me into the light where I have found freedom in you. I commit my spirit to you and pray you continue to direct my every step as you counsel and teach me your ways.

From God: This time He led me to a scripture reminding me He is teaching me all things when I seek Him with all my heart and soul.

I will instruct you and teach you in the way you should go; I will counsel you with my loving eye on you (Psalms 32:8 NIV).

. . . .

Encouraging Word from God—2017

The Lord shared and wanted to teach me at the time not to fear my assignment. He said, *there is no fear in failure, only a lesson to learn.* Not to fear doing something right or wrong—there is no right or wrong way in the Kingdom, Only His way. Not to fear steeping out of our comfort zone is how we go higher with Him. Not to fear or doubt if I am hearing Him correctly, which caused me to stay parked waiting on Him. There are times to wait and pray, and times to move in trust. He reminded me His sheep know His voice, *so why do you not follow the path I set before you?* Remember the thief comes to steal, kill, and destroy. I came to give you life. He said, DO NOT FEAR I AM WITH YOU AND WILL GIVE YOU ALL YOU NEED TO FULFILL THE PLANS I HAVE FOR YOU! Get ready!

He has great plans for all of us. We can say we are willing, but are we willing to act? Go out of our comfort zone? Take a risk and trust in Him? His word tells us to be doers, not just hearers of the word. *Good things are not all God things.* Those can be distractions that detour us. Obstacles will come, but it is in those times we are learning as He navigates us through.

You make know to me the path of life; you will fill me with joy in your presence, with eternal pleasures at your right hand (Psalm 16:11 NKJV).

. . . .

Cast your Burden—2020

Is your backpack too heavy for you to carry any longer? Is it filled with anxiety, fear, stress, feeling overwhelmed, anger, and depression? Jesus wants to be a friend who walks alongside you and carries your backpack. Let Him carry it today, and cast ALL your burdens upon Him.

Cast your burden on the Lord, (release it) and He will sustain and uphold you; He will never allow the righteous to be shaken (slip, fall, fail) (Psalms 55:22 AMP).

These scriptures have changed my life. I have learned to stand on them daily, letting them change me from the inside out. God loves to speak to each one of us individually. One of these might resonate with you. He will show you one. I encourage you as you seek to go deeper into God's word, look for the scriptures that stop you in your tracks or feel like God's giving you a big hug. Those are times God is speaking into your life so you too can have scriptures to Stand On and Stand Up with.

Romans 12:2 (NKJV)
And do not conform to the patterns of this world, but be transformed by the renewing of your mind, that you may prove what is that good and acceptable and perfect will of God.

Psalm 16:1 (TPT)
Keep me safe, O mighty God. I run to you, my safe place.

Jeremiah 29:11 (NKJV)
For I know the thoughts that I think toward you, says the Lord, thoughts of peace and not of evil, to give you a future and a hope.

2 Timothy 1:7 (NKJV)
For God has not given us a spirit of fear, but of power (Holy Spirit), Love (the father) and of a sound mind (the mind of Christ).

Psalm 119-105 (NKJV)
Your word is a lamp to my feet and a light to my path.

Romans 12:12 (NKJV)
Rejoicing in hope, patient in tribulation, continuing steadfastly in prayer.

Psalm 20:4 (NKJV)
May He grant you according to your heart's desire. And fulfill all your purpose.

Psalm 141:3 (NKJV)
Set a guard, O Lord, over my mouth, Keep watch over the door of my lips.

Romans 8:1 (NKJV)
There is therefore now no condemnation to those who are in Christ Jesus, who do not walk according to the Flesh, but according to the Spirit.

Psalms 32:8 (NIV)

I will instruct you and teach you in the way you should go; I will counsel you with my loving eye on you.

1 Peter 4:12 (NKJV)

Beloved do not think it strange concerning the fiery trial which is to try you, as though some strange thing happened to you, but rejoice to the extent that you partake of Christ suffering, that when His glory is received, you may also be glad with exceeding joy.

Psalm 34:18 (NIV)

The Lord is close to the brokenhearted and saves those who are crushed in spirit

Romans 13:14 (NKJV)

Put on the Lord Jesus Christ, and make no provision for the flesh, to fulfill its lust

Psalm 139:13-14 (NKJV)

For You formed my inward parts: You covered me in my mother's womb. I will praise You, for I am fearfully and wonderfully made; Marvelous are your works, and that my soul knows very well.

1 John 4:4 (NKJV)

You are of God, little children, and have overcome, because He who is in you is greater than he who is in the world.

Psalm 84:11 (TPT)

For the Lord God is brighter than the brilliance of sunrise! Wrapping himself around me like a shield, he is so generous with his gifts of grace and glory. Those who walk along his paths with integrity will never lack one thing they need, for he provides it all!

Psalm 86:13 (TPT)

You loved me so much you placed your greatness upon me. You rescued me from the deepest place of darkness, and you have delivered me from certain death.

Psalm 81:16 (TPT)

But I will feed you with my spiritual bread. You will feast and be satisfied with me, feeding on my revelation-truth like honey dripping from the cliffs of the high place.

· ·

Go Deeper—Stand up

Create your own Journal Entry and speak whatever is in your heart. He already knows and is not looking for perfection either.

Then sit still and listen to His reply. If you don't hear anything at first that it is okay. It will take practice like anything. Remember He might just speak a word; give you a song or a scripture to look up. **Trust in the process!**

PRAYER

Lord I pray that you open the eyes of my heart to hear ONLY you so that I will gain the understanding and knowledge of all that you want to share with me.

Date:
Dear God,

From God

NOTES

CHAPTER 6

Run with Christ

My life has taken many turns, but it has all ended in the arms of my loving Father in Heaven. He has given His life for mine so that I can be FREE. The JOY in knowing that brings a LOVE over me that can't be described, only felt! He is constantly reminding me of His love, and at times it has overwhelmed me. I have such joy that I want to shout to the world, "GOD LOVES YOU!"

I have a deep passion and desire to share with you what God has freely given to me. My prayer is that you would come to know Jesus as your savior, grow in your relationship with Him, and be overwhelmed by His love. He is the most loving person I know. Even on days when I have missed the mark, I know He is working it all out for my good, because of the deep love I have for Him. Sometimes we are not ready to receive what He has for us until we can gain the understanding of what He's doing in us and for us. I know that God is always working in our favor behind the scenes. When we are ready, we can embrace all that He has for us. God has many lessons He wants to teach us. I now have learned to see and celebrate the increase in those lessons, even the smallest ones.

The Lord has brought times of discipline and lessons in my life. Today I can truly say I celebrate those moments of correction and changes that He has brought into my life. Some were not easy to look at. The enemy tried to confuse me with condemnation, causing me to feel worthless. Now I can see when it was God and His correction. It takes time to learn the difference between the two. Just know that God does not bring shame and guilt, making you dislike yourself. He brings a gentle, yet clear, correction that causes you to feel remorse with a desire to repent changing your ways.

The Father, Jesus, and the Holy Spirit are all living in me. I am comforted by that, knowing I'm never alone. God's promise tells us. He has left the Holy Spirit with us to be our helper in all things. *The Helper, Holy Spirit, whom the Father will send in My name, He will teach you all things, and being to your remembrance all things that I said to you. Peace I leave with you, My peace I give to you; not as the world gives do I give to you. Let not your heart be troubled neither let it be afraid* (John 14:26-28 NKJV).

Now I no longer want to settle. I want to become the best version that God created me to be. God has shared with me that I must practice and apply what I have learned, so it can penetrate deep within my heart where the change takes place. As I learn to apply it correctly, I can walk it out, not think it out, in His will and ways. If I don't practice what He is teaching me, I cannot walk out ALL that He has for me.

Then the next lesson appears, and that looks different for all of us. Sometimes it takes a few tries to get it right. Nothing comes easily as we grow in our desire to want to change. Thankfully God is patient, loving and kind walking along side us as we journey with Him through the process of maturing in Christ. Sometimes I run and don't walk. He says it is okay to "run along but not ahead" as He is my life's running partner.

The more I have encountered God, the more I long to seek and know Him. It takes time and being intentional to grow closer. That is my daily desire. I am so thankful for His love and the transformation He has brought me through.

Early in my walk with God He used butterflies to remind me He was with me. Think of the transformation of a butterfly and the struggle it goes through as a worm in the cocoon only to come out a beautiful butterfly. That is what we look like when we first come to Him in our brokenness. Through His love, grace, and mercy, He shines His beauty through our cocoon cage creating a beautiful masterpiece in us. When I changed my thinking to kingdom thinking I gained a better understanding of who I am in Christ. It is not who the world says I am. Only then was I able to sit, stand, walk, and then run in the confidence as His Beloved Daughter!

I continue to walk, following my heart and God's direction for my journey. He began to open many doors and close others. I have to be willing to cooperate with Him in order to live according to the destiny

He has willed for my life. God gives us passions and desires. It is up to us to live and walk out His plan. Every seed God plants in us is an opportunity for Him to water it so we can bear good fruit in our lives. In order to bear good fruit, you must prepare to be cut and pruned like a tree. God wants to cut off the limbs that are dead so you can blossom.

Run to your destiny and all that He has for you. Do what is right, not allowing your emotions to tell you different. Too many times we let our emotions dictate how we feel. It is in those times we just need to keep moving forward keeping our eyes on Jesus even when we don't feel like it.

God shared with me, "To be in action you must take action." Today take the action to run and overcome with Christ. Every time you step forward you will overcome. Depression, anxiety and negativity only give the enemy power to steal your joy. When we feel defeated, allowing negative thoughts to overtake us, it gives the enemy the power to take us out of Gods plan. Don't allow the enemy to keep you in the dark. It is not always the enemy that causes us to stumble but a Christian who can't understand or deal in their emotions.

There were many times that I was too weak to overcome my emotions. One day the Lord presented a flower to me. I thanked Him and also asked why. He said as the petals fall to the ground, so should your emotions fall to me. That is when I started to learn to live from my inner spirit, not my emotions, letting all things rise in me allowing **the joy of the Lord to be my strength.** Run into the arms of Jesus so you can come out of your trauma and trouble, learning and gaining the strength to walk in your healing, only to be able to go higher with Him.

Today I run, holding His hand as He leads the way. I take time to sit still with Him to hear His assignments. There are times when I am not sure if I have heard Him correctly. It is in those moments when I STAND patiently until I hear a clear *yes or no* in my spirit, not in my mind. Other times I have to proceed forward, trusting in His plan. It's in those times that I have peace, that I know it is God. If I did not have peace or felt rushed, I knew it was not from God.

I used to jump into things, only to find they were not part of His plan for me. I eventually learned that not all good things are God things.

I learned to be careful to not to get distracted. Distraction and focus are part of the learning process. The enemy would love to keep us distracted from our true walk and destiny with God. I heard the Lord say "keep climbing and seeking the steps I lay out for you. Soon you will reach the top of the mountain gaining your wings to fly, where I will stretch, grow and mature you. Press forward and step into all that I have for you."

God is calling us all to press in so we can press forward. God cannot move a parked car. Those were wise words from one of my teachers that became a revelation to walk without fear but in Faith! His word tells us He goes before us to prepare the way. Can you Trust in Him and believe so you can walk the path He has laid out for you? ***He goes before you; He will be with you every step of the way never leaving you*** (Deuteronomy 31:8 NKJV). When I look back, He did prepare the way and still is!

. . . .

Going Deeper—Run with Christ

Are you running to God or away from God?

What is causing you to run from God?

Will you choose today to run with Christ? Sometimes you have to crawl before you can walk and then run. He is waiting with open arms.

PRAYER

Lord, I thank you that you give us the strength to run when we are weak. Knowing we can come to you as we are! I thank you that you are not looking for me to be perfect but to walk with a desire to be more Christlike. YOU already died on the Cross for it all! We walk in freedom with full assurance as your beloved sons and daughters. We run with endurance strengthened by Christ explosive power to conquer and overcome all difficulty. We are more than conquers!

In the darkest moments when you feel you can't go on, dig deep into your spirit and lean in knowing that God is right there by your side. Search your heart and listen for His still small voice that is inviting you to step into His loving arms. He wants to bring you out of darkness and into His light. God wants us to take His hand and run with Him. Let Him lead the way. Let your light shine bright for all to see the battle you have overcome with Him. Make a decision today to run to Him. He is waiting with open arms. **You are an Over Comer!** *For everyone born of God is victorious and overcomes the world; and this is the victory that has conquered and overcome the world-our continuing persistent faith in Jesus the son of God* (1 John 5:4).

RUN WITH CHRIST AND OVERCOME

Replace Depression with Joy: For the Joy of the Lord is your strength (Nehemiah 8:10 NKJV)

Replace Defeat with Victory: Thanks be to God who gives us victory through our Lord Jesus Christ (1 Corinthians 15:57 NKJV)

Replace Denial with Truth: Jesus said I am the way, the truth and the life. No one comes to the father except though me (John 14:6 NKJV)

Replace Insecurity with Confidence: For I am confident of this very thing, that He who began a good work in you will perfect it until the day of Christ Jesus (Philippians 1:6 NKJV)

Replace Obsession with Contentment: Now godliness with contentment is great gain (1 Timothy 6:6 NKJV)

NOTES:

CHAPTER 7

Steady Peace

Today I look back and see that He went before me and prepared the way for where I am in my journey now. I always had a desire to help others through my testimony. I know there is hope for every lost little girl because I once was lost. Jesus rescued me and has grown me to be a woman with a heart and passion to share God's love with others, so they too can know how worthy and LOVED they are by Him. There is freedom that awaits us when we surrender our hearts and turn our lives over to Christ. Repentance is important, so our sins can be forgiven, and we can turn things around. Repentance requires us to feel truly broken. It is NOT asking the Lord to forgive with the intent to sin again but with an honest regretful heart that acknowledges our sin with a desired commitment to want to change. When I realized that, I no longer was a captive! I grew in a love and gratitude for Christ that I can't put into words. With the help of the Holy Spirit my passion turned into a fire to encourage and share God, His word and His never-ending love for us that brings steady peace to our lives. That's when He shared Isaiah 61:1.

I had no idea what that meant when He spoke it to me back in 2014. He then led me to His word in Isaiah 61:1 NLT which says, *"The Spirit of the Lord God is upon me, because the Lord has anointed me to bring the good news to the poor. He has sent me to comfort the brokenhearted to proclaim captives will be released and prisoners will be freed."* I trusted and waited for I knew He would explain.

It was in 2016 that He revealed His plan. An opportunity came my way to go to a retreat by myself with the Lord. I felt called to the secret place. In that place I started to write, and that is when the Lord birthed in me The Daughters of Eve. He gave me content for a six-week journey that would help young teen girls find their true identity in Christ, setting them free of all that held them bondage. I spent three glorious days with the Lord with no distractions or internet. He dictated and I wrote. We took long walks on the trails, worshiped, prayed, and rested together. I felt so blessed.

It didn't happen overnight. It took three years to bring to life. In the process I learned more about myself and how God wanted me to walk with Him. When God gives us His vision for our life it takes time! Be patient. Seek Him in the process. Don't give up! It starts in our heart and slowly He directs our path of learning the process so we can achieve greatness for His glory and the good of His Kingdom. *My word is a lamp to your feet and a light to your path* (Psalm 119:105 NKJV).

When the Daughters of Eve first started out, it was at my church in the high school ministry. It was a great place to start. Soon after, I sensed God wanted me to speak into those held captive and in chains, the ones that were lost and hurting and still seeking to know Him. When I started out some days no one showed up. A leader mentioned, *but you showed up and that is what God wants to see. Can He entrust you with His plan?* Those words impact me still to this day. I knew I was being called to the teens who were struggling in our detention centers, but how was that to work out?

One day I prayed and asked the Lord to guide me. He told me to reach out to my city's detention center. A few months went by and one morning I awoke. "Today is the day He said." It was 8:30 in the morning. I called, expecting to be put off or have no answer. The telephone rang, and then I heard a lovely woman's voice. I knew God's hand and favor was upon it. It all fell into place so easily. Today Daughters of Eve has become more of a prison ministry, consisting of a five-week journey learning how to grow in a relationship with our Heavenly Father. Learning and knowing how to walk worthy of His love in order to surrender their hearts to the true identity, building faith, and strength with His word of truth. This sets a captive free and allows her the confidence to walk in who she is: His Beloved Daughter.

Our prayer today is to stay humble so God can use us throughout our city to bring the good news that will touch and change the lives of young teen girls, so they may become and believe all that they were created to be in His image. His word tells us He will never abandon us—no matter what. He wants to take our rags and make beautiful garments out of them.

That is my mission - to bring the hope of God, drawing others to a place of believing in Him and themselves, as someone once did for me. Do you have dreams and desires that God has placed in your heart? Are you waiting on God, or is He waiting on you? I know fear can try to come in and stop us from walking out what God is calling us to. Seek Him in those dreams and desires and see how He will lead you. Remember, all good things are not God things. If it is God, He will give you the strength and peace to step out. He always directs our path when we are willing. You might be nervous and have butterflies in your stomach, but be encouraged that He will give you the courage to walk it out. It's not through our own strength, but through His, that we are able to fulfill our assignments and purpose. We were made by God for Great Things!

Going Deeper—Steady Peace

Below are some examples of who God is and wants to be for me. Knowing I can call on him to be all things has brought steady peace in my life.

WHO IS HE IS FOR YOU THAT WILL STEADY YOUR PEACE?

He is my savior: **Act 4:12**

He is my protector: **Psalm 18:2**

He is my loving Father: **1 John 3:1**

He is my joy: **Nehemiah 8:10**

He is my confidence: **1 John 3 20-22**

He is my patience: **2 Peter 3:9**

He is my compassion: **Matthew 9:36**

He is my best friend: **Song of Solomon 5:16**

He is my encourager: **Romans 15:13**

He is my provider: **Philippians 4:19**

He is my peace: **Colossians 3:15**

He is the bind that holds my marriage: **Zechariah 2:5**

He is my counselor: **Psalm 32:8**

He is my teacher: **John 14:26**

He is my Heart: **Psalm 34:18**

PRAYER

Thank you, Jesus, that you are so many things for me. Thank you that I can call on you and your promises that steady my peace of who You say You are keeping me rooted and grounded in your love.

NOTES

CHAPTER 8

His Invitation

You might ask why a person would desire to give their life to God. That desire is sometimes called *longing*. That longing may feel like a pull or nudge in our spirit. We can be unsure at times what that pull might be until He shows up in our struggle and calls us by name, putting a pause on our life because we know someone is talking to us. Have you sensed God talking to you and calling you by your name? GOD calls us to come in our dirty rags and all, even when we think *how can God forgive me?* We no longer have to suffer. He already suffered and died for all our sins on the cross. He wants to rescue us from death and destruction, even when we are rebelling against Him or hating Him! He desires fellowship with us. He is not looking for perfection - only your heart's desire to love and a willingness to walk with Him. He chose to give His life because of the goodness and value He created us for. Salvation is His gift to us. He died so we can be made pure, blameless and spotless in our hearts before God.

He demonstrated this love for us while we were still sinners by giving His Son's life (Romans 5:8 NKJV). THINK ABOUT THAT!

Jesus wants to be our Savior. His name means Deliver, to save. He wants to be everything for us. He wants to break off the desires of our flesh which tempt us and lead us down the wrong path. He wants to heal our broken hearts, carry our burdens, and heal our wounds, making us whole in Him. God does not force Himself on us. He pursues us and leads with His unconditional love.

God is not far off. He's right there, inviting you to sit at the table with Him. Are you willing and ready to accept His invitation and let Him embrace you with His love that will never fail you? Are you feeling broken, lost, alone, depressed, and anxious? Or have you turned away, only to hear Him calling you back? He offers us a life of freedom. Free from ourselves. We are given our own free will and a choice to choose life in Him or death if we remain in the worldly things. I choose life! How about you?

Do you want to invite God to come into your life today? He paid the ultimate price for you with His life.How does it make you feel to know He freely gave His life for you? *We love God, not because we are supposed to, but because He first loved us.* (1 John 4:19 NKJV). His love nurtures us like a parent who nurtures a newborn baby. As we grow up, we grow more in love and desire for Him. Are there lies you believe that are keeping you from surrendering your life and accepting His invitation? If so, bring them before Him, examine your heart. Then take the step to be Free in Him.

If you desire to accept His invitation of salvation and His love so you can walk in the wholeness and fullness Jesus has to offer you, I invite you to say this prayer. Or maybe you have accepted His invitation but walked away from God. I invite you to repent and recommit your heart. Let His love wash over you today, washing away all your sins so you can start to walk out your journey as a new creation in Christ.

PRAYER

Lord, today I accept you as my Lord and Savior. I thank you for dying on the cross for my sins. I surrender my life and ask you to forgive me of all my sins and invite you into my heart. I choose life and freedom in you. Make me the person you created me to be, in Jesus' Name. Amen.

If you prayed that, welcome to the family, heaven is rejoicing over you. He is so excited to develop a relationship with you. He delights in you. As we become more intimate with Him in fellowship and begin to read His word our peace, joy, and love for Him will increase. He doesn't promise better days. He promises a brand-new life.

He doesn't make it better—He makes you better.

But to all who did receive Him, who believed in His name He gave the right to become children of God, who were born, not of blood or of the will of the flesh, or of the will of man, but of God. (John 1:12-13 NKJV)

. . . .

Going Deeper—His Invitation to Know Him More

What are some ways that you would get to know a friend? God wants us to develop our relationship with Him the Father, Jesus and the Holy Spirit. Our joy will increase as we become more intimate in fellowship and friendship with Him.

What is the first way that you will want to start getting to know God?

Talk or write a letter to Him, start journaling daily. Ask Him questions and engage. He will answer. Share all that you are feeling and going through. He wants to be everything for you.

My heart has an overwhelming love for the Father, Son and Holy Spirit. Over the years my desire for and relationship with the Lord has grown in a way that I never could have imagined. I fall more in love with Him every day. My journey has been one of growing in His heart and in His love for me. No matter what, I can remain in Him, abiding where I can rest and find peace.

My prayer for you is that He will capture your heart in such a way that you will be overwhelmed with His love and bring you into your salvation. It will change your life forever! I hope if you are reading this and struggle in any area of your life, you will find the help and support needed to make a change. There is hope for everyone. Some get more chances than others. Hopefully it's the one that saves and changes your life bringing the Freedom that Jesus offers to you. I was fortunate. Some are NOT!

The Lord your God is in your midst, The Mighty One, will save; He will rejoice over you with gladness, He will quiet you with His love, He will exalt over you with singing. (Zephaniah 3:17 NKJV)

Blessing to you all as you embark on your journey with Jesus. It's the best journey every travel!

—Jill

About the Author

Jill Kaczmarowski is the Founder and Executive Director of the Daughters of Eve ministry. She is a trained volunteer peer counselor with the Eve Center, an entrepreneur, blogger and a dedicated wife and mother.

As a Christian woman, Jill has a deep desire and passion to help young teenage girls discover their true identity in Christ. She has a heart to encourage and empower these girls, so they can grow into the beautiful, strong, and confident women they were created to be. Through her own struggles as a teen, Jill has answered the call on her life and is dedicated to helping teenage girls find hope, healing and freedom only found in Christ Jesus. It is in the personal relationship she developed with Jesus, that His love, grace and LIVING WORD transformed her. She believes when we truly surrender our hearts to Jesus we are set FREE anchored His Love that changes us from the inside out. Jill has such a love for God that in her story you can hear how He brought her out of darkness and into His glorious light. She is ever thankful for all He has done and continues to do in and through her life.

Visit the Daughters of Eve online at:
thedaughtersofeve.org

CPSIA information can be obtained
at www.ICGtesting.com
Printed in the USA
FSHW020824021121

9 781970 063769